BURYING GENERAL BROCK

A HISTORY OF BROCK'S MONUMENTS

Robert Malcomson

The Friends of Fort George

Copyright © Robert Malcomson 1996

All rights reserved. No part of this publication may be reproduced, stored in a retrieval system, or transmitted in any form or by any means, electronic, mechanical, photocopying, recording, or otherwise (except brief passages for purposes of review) without the prior permission of the author and The Friends of Fort George.

Printed and bound in Canada by Peninsula Press.

Care has been taken to trace the ownership of copyright material used in the text (including the illustrations.) The author and the publisher welcome any information enabling them to rectify any reference or credit in subsequent editions.

Front cover illustration: Portrait of Major General Sir Isaac Brock by J. W. L. Forster (1850-1938). Unless otherwise indicated, photographs in this book were taken by the author.

Canadian Cataloguing in Publication Data

Malcomson, Robert, 1949-
 Burying General Brock: A history of Brock's monuments

Includes bibliographical references and index.
ISBN 0-9699298-1-1

1. Brock, Isaac, Sir, 1769-1812--Monuments.
2. Brock, Isaac, Sir, 1769-1812--Death and burials.
3. Queenston Heights (Ont.), Battle of, 1812. I. Friends of Fort George. II. Title.

FC443.B76M34 1996   971.03'4   C96-900189-4
E353.1.B8M34 1996

Foreword

Is General Brock buried under the monument? That may sound like the old query about who's buried in Grant's Tomb, but it is one I have heard from young and old alike. This book was written to answer the question and to tell the rather complex story of the homage paid to the famous soldier. Who would have thought that it would take forty-one years to lay Brock and his assistant to rest?

This book was funded by a grant from Parks Canada and The Friends of Fort George. The proceeds of its sale will go entirely to the support of employment opportunities managed by The Friends at Parks Canada sites in Niagara.

Research was conducted at the following institutions: the National Archives of Canada, the National Library of Canada, the Ontario Archives, the Metropolitan Toronto Reference Library, the Special Collections Room at the Brock University Library, the public libraries in St. Catharines and Niagara-on-the-Lake, the Lundy's Lane Museum and the Niagara Historical Museum.

Thanks are extended to Dennis Skowronski for the use of the printer on his desk and to Des Morris, of Peninsula Press, for his creative contributions in the production of the book.

Jim Alexander read an early version of the manuscript and made encouraging comments about it. Dennis Gannon used his editor's eye to identify the flaws that needed correction. Dennis also provided research materials and support throughout the project. Carrie Malcomson read a draft and offered her valuable insights. Melanie and Janet Malcomson helped to weed out the last of the miscues. To all these people the author expresses his gratitude, and happily lets them off the hook for any errors that remain.

**This book is dedicated to
Erika and Jim Alexander,
the heart and soul of The Friends of Fort George**

The fatal bullet hole in the "plain coatee" worn by Isaac Brock at Queenston Heights is evident in this photograph taken in 1896. The jacket was actually a well-used one that Brock wore while he was a brigadier general. *(Courtesy of the Notman Photographic Archives, McCord Museum.)*

THE DEATH OF ISAAC BROCK

    Major General Isaac Brock was shot by an American soldier on the hillside below Queenston Heights early on the morning of Tuesday, 13 October 1812.
    The battle at Queenston had been raging for a couple of hours by that time. After some initial success, the American invasion force had been pinned down on the shore of the Niagara River by well-directed British fire. In an attempt to outflank the British, about one hundred and fifty American infantrymen under the command of Captain John Wool of the 13th U. S. Regiment had scaled the gorge wall further upriver. Wool's men then seized the 18-pounder gun in the redan battery located halfway up the shoulder of the escarpment.
    Pushing the Americans away from their "high ground" position as quickly as possible was vitally important, so General Brock rallied about 50 men and led the charge up the slope. He did not get very far.
    Robert Walcot claimed to be the marksman who killed Isaac Brock. He was a private in one of the companies that had followed Captain Wool to capture the redan battery. Wanting to help stem the British counter-attack, he borrowed a loaded musket from one of his mates and rammed a second ball down its smooth-bore barrel. "I went to the edge of the line," Walcot testified, "and, taking aim, fired at Brock. His face was partly turned to the troops as I fired. He fell almost instantly."[1]
    George Jarvis, a volunteer with the Light Company of the 49th Regiment, was following just behind Brock when the American bullet struck Brock in the chest. "Our gallant General fell on his left side within a few feet of where I stood," recollected Jarvis. "Running up to him I enquired, 'Are you much hurt, Sir?' He placed his hand on his breast and made no reply."[2]
    As the attack against the Americans was renewed by his followers, Brock's body was carried off the field and hidden in

a house in the village. A portion of the village later fell into the hands of the Americans, but the corpse was not discovered. After Major General Roger Hale Sheaffe had organized a resounding British victory late in the afternoon, Captain John Glegg, one of Brock's aides-de-camp, hurried to retrieve the general's body and transport it to Niagara (modern-day Niagara-on-the-Lake).

Government House at Niagara had been Isaac Brock's headquarters while he was in the Niagara Peninsula, and it was there that he was laid in state on 14 October, "bedewed by the tears of many affectionate friends."[3] He was soon joined by one of his friends. Lieutenant Colonel John Macdonell, the 27-year-old attorney general of Upper Canada, and colonial aide-de-camp to Brock, had pressed the attack to recapture the redan battery after the general fell, but he, too, was shot. Felled by a mortal wound through his abdomen, Macdonell clung to life at Government House until 1:30 a.m. on the fourteenth when he succumbed.

John Macdonell was 27 years old at the time of his death. He was the attorney general of Upper Canada. He was also a lieutenant colonel in the province's militia and was serving as Brock's provincial aide-de-camp. This silhouette of him was made around 1810.
(Courtesy of the Metropolitan Toronto Reference Library, J. Ross Robertson Collection, T17053)

16 OCTOBER 1812
THE FIRST BURIAL

Major General Sheaffe and his staff officers decided that Macdonell would be buried with his chief and that Captain Glegg would manage the funeral arrangements. Glegg went to work on the lavish preparations. His formal order, issued on 16 October, the day of the funeral, specified the roles to be played by each of the numerous groups and individuals involved. Detachments from the regular army and the militia and Indian corps were to line each side of the route that stretched from Government House to Fort George. The Royal Artillery Regiment was directed to fire the traditional minute guns with a pair of nine-pounders. All officers were required to wear black arm bands and black crepe on their sword knots during the funeral; the arm bands continued to be worn for the next month.[4]

Glegg also arranged for a local silversmith to inscribe plates that could be fixed to the caskets. It was later reported that Brock's inscription read:

Here lie the earthly remains of a brave and virtuous Hero, Major General Sir Isaac Brock, Commanding the British Forces, and President Administering the Government of Upper Canada, who fell when gloriously engaging the enemies of his Country at the head of the Flank Companies of the 49th Regiment in the Town of Queenston, on the morning of the 13th Oct. 1812. Aged 42 yrs. J. B. Glegg A. D. C.[5]

At 10:00 a. m. on Friday, 16 October the funeral procession got underway when Fort Major Campbell led the slow march from Government House, followed by a company from the 41st Regiment and a company of militiamen. Next came the band of the 41st Regiment playing a dirge, its drums muffled and draped in black cloth. Brock's horse, decorated

The first resting place of General Brock and his assistant, John Macdonell, was the bastion in the northeast corner of Fort George. A stone marking the spot is visible in the centre of this photograph.

with ornamental coverings, was led by four grooms, after which came three groups: the general's personal servants, four surgeons and the chaplain at Fort George, the Reverend Mr. Robert Addison.

    A team of horses drew the first caisson with the casket containing the body of Lieutenant Colonel Macdonell, attended by six pall bearers and three mourners, the foremost of whom was Alexander Macdonell, brother to the slain officer. Brock's caisson followed, accompanied by nine pall bearers: Major Evans, Captains Glegg, Dennis, Holcroft and Vigoreaux, and militia officers Claus, Butler, Powell and Merritt. Major General Sheaffe was among the general's official mourners, who were followed by staff from the provincial government, Brock's civilian friends and the general public.

    A single grave had been dug in the newly-constructed bastion in the northeast corner of Fort George. When the caskets were placed at the graveside and the notables had gathered in and around the bastion, Reverend Addison read the service and the two caskets were lowered into the grave.[6] At that point a twenty-one-gun salute was fired in three salvoes of seven guns each. It was echoed at sunset by a similar salute offered by the Americans at Fort Niagara.

"No pen can describe the real scenes of that mournful day," wrote Captain Glegg. "A more solemn and affecting spectacle was, perhaps, never witnessed."[7] The funeral of Isaac Brock and John Macdonell was attended by thousands, which indicated the regard in which the general had been held. Among those deeply affected by his shocking and heroic death was Ann Bruyeres, the daughter of a prominent lieutenant colonel in the corps of Royal Engineers. The young woman put a quill to paper to express her sorrow in a poem that ended with: "Glory threw on his grave a laurel wreath, and Fame proclaims, 'A hero sleeps beneath.'"[8]

Within weeks another symbol was laid on Brock's grave. On 6 November members from the Six Nations, Huron, Chippewa and Potawatomie tribes met at the Council House at Fort George. William Claus, Deputy Superintendent of the Indian Department, was present, as was Captain John Norton, who had played a significant role in frustrating the American invasion at Queenston. Chief Kodeaneyonte made a speech and gave Major General Sheaffe and his staff the gift of eight strings of white wampum "to wipe away your tears." He also presented to the British a large, white wampum belt to cover Brock's grave so that his remains "would receive no injury."[9]

There was foresight in the Indian gift. In May 1813 Fort George fell into American hands where it remained until the following December. When he finally arrived at the recaptured garrison, John Glegg was relieved to discover that Brock and Macdonell's grave had been left undisturbed by the invaders.

ISAAC BROCK'S ESTATE

General Brock's worldly possessions were distributed in several different ways. An itemized list, fifteen pages in length, was prepared showing a large number of his belongings and who bought them.[10] Major General Sheaffe bought the majority of the collection, spending £602 for items ranging from a mustard pot and spoon to a bedroom carpet and more than 200 bottles of wines, beers and spirits. John Glegg spent £15 on a cream pot, pillow cases and two dozen bottles of port. Glegg also paid £5 for a bedstead, which was to be given to a Mrs. Brown, without explanation.

On 4 January 1813 an auction was held to dispense with the remaining articles, which raised £329. Brock's library, stocked with volumes like "Expeditions to Holland," "Elegant

A major general's "dress coatee" was presented by Brock's grandnieces, Henrietta and Emilia Tupper, to David Ross McCord in 1909. *(Courtesy of the Notman Photographic Archives, McCord Museum)*

Extracts" and "Johnson's Dictionary," went to buyers including the Reverend Dr. John Strachan and other leading citizens of the province.

Captain Glegg kept some of the general's personal belongings so that they could be returned to his family. In the spring of 1813, Brock's chief servant, Thomas Porter, delivered them to the Brock family at their home on the Isle of Guernsey in the English Channel. Among the articles were a dress tunic, a sash, a cravat and an undress coatee, presumed to be the jacket that Brock wore at the time of his death. The Brock family kept the items until the turn of the century when the general's grandnieces decided to present them to Canadian institutions.

Following his friend's death, John Glegg assured William Brock that he had been "intimately acquainted . . . with your Brother's sentiments on the most private subjects, and can take upon me to say he has left no natural child for your care."[11] There was, however, a young boy living under the general's roof. Glegg only identified him as a ten-year-old named Ellis, who Brock had taken in after his father, a captain in the 49th Regiment, had drowned in passage from Canada around 1809. Glegg explained that he had placed young Ellis in a good school and that he was well cared for.

THE FIRST MONUMENT

Although Brock's death was universally mourned in Canada, it was his homeland that sponsored the first monument to his memory. The British Parliament passed a bill on 20 July 1813 requiring that a suitable memorial be erected in the memory of the general who had "died to preserve what Wolfe died to gain."[12] The contract was awarded to Richard Westmacott, an officer in the Royal Artillery and a sculptor of some renown, who produced a bas-relief "military monument" at a cost of £1,575. It was mounted high on the wall in the west ambulatory of the south transept of St. Paul's Cathedral in London, where Vice Admiral Lord Horatio Nelson and other great British heroes had already been laid to rest. The sculpture shows Brock lying dead in the arms of a British soldier while a native warrior looks on with respect.

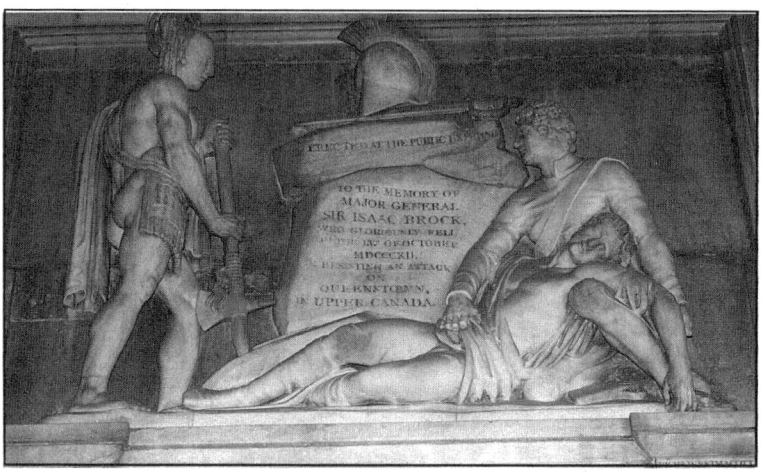

Richard Westmacott's monument to Major General Brock is located on the main floor of St. Paul's Cathedral in London, England. Nearby are the tombs of Britain's most famous warriors, including Lord Nelson and the Duke of Wellington.

To honour the family of the general, the Prince Regent ordered that a grant of 12,000 acres of land in Upper Canada be given to Brock's four surviving brothers and that they each receive a yearly pension of £200.

The people of Guernsey also honoured Brock. An oak screen was constructed in the parish church of St. Peter Port and dedicated by the Bishop of Winchester. A simple inscription was added to the screen: "Sir Isaac Brock, K. B. Who Saved Canada."[13]

THE FIRST TOWER ON QUEENSTON HEIGHTS

The legislature for the province of Upper Canada was not long in following the lead of the imperial government. In March 1814 a motion was passed "to commemorate the great and brilliant services" of the general, and a sum of £500 was appropriated "for the purpose of erecting a monument on the heights of Queenstown near the spot where he fell."[14]

The following March the provincial parliament voted that the sum be raised to £1000 and a committee was selected to steer the project. Robert Nichol, who had made the original proposal to honour Brock, was appointed to the committee as were two other prominent veterans and public officials, Thomas Dickson and Thomas Clark. One of the first things the commissioners did was to write a letter to William Brock asking for his family's opinion on what kind of memorial would be most appropriate. They assured him that they did not expect to be restricted to the fund set up by the province since a flood of private subscriptions would undoubtedly supplement it.[15]

It was two years before a response arrived from the general's family. William Brock finally wrote in 1817 to explain that the family had asked Richard Westmacott to prepare a suitable design. The sculptor devised such an extravagant plan that the Brocks decided it would be best for one of their representatives to present it in person. John Savery Brock carried Westmacott's plan to Canada and visited Thomas Dickson at Niagara in August 1817. The proposal showed a 2.5 metre (eight feet) tall bronze statue of the general standing atop a granite pedestal and base, around which were placed reliefs of his actions at Detroit and Queenston. The monument would stand 5.6 metres (18 feet, 6 inches) tall and could be constructed for £2500, inclusive of shipment costs; a smaller monument was estimated to cost about £2000.

Despite the advice they received from the Brocks, the

commissioners made little progress on their task. Late in 1821 they reported to the legislature about the Westmacott plan, but admitted that fund-raising from subscribers had not been very successful. The building account stood at about £1500, due mainly to interest earned on the original amount, which had been invested successfully.

Two other plans for towers to be erected on the heights above Queenston were presented for the commissioners' consideration. One showed a column with a funeral urn at its peak, similar to the Nelson Monument constructed in Montreal in 1809. The second plan, depicting a taller and more elaborate tower with a mausoleum for Brock's remains, was favoured as "a more appropriate testimonial of the Strong feeling of veneration" held by the government and people.[16]

The presumed strong feelings of veneration did not increase the flow of donations to the building fund, however. By January 1824 less than £2000 had been amassed. A suggestion had been put forward to scale down the project; a chapel with a memorial, marble tablet set into one of its walls could be built on the Heights. The Brocks had commented in a letter that the family would be satisfied with that simpler commemoration.[17]

Nichol, Dickson and Clark urged the government to remain true to the initial aims of its legislation. In the fall of 1823 they advertised in local newspapers for submissions from interested parties for a circular tower of cut stone, measuring 15.5 metres (50 feet) high and 4.8 metres (16 feet) wide with a winding staircase inside. In February 1824 the commissioners reported that they had selected one of the two proposals they had received. It was a Tuscan column designed by an engineer named Francis Hall who estimated his fee at about £2200.[18]

The project got underway at Queenston during the late spring of 1824. A site was cleared on "a kind of promontory directly overhanging the main street of Queenston and not in the way of any military work."[19] Francis Hall supervised the digging of a foundation and the delivery of building stone from

From the exterior observation deck on Brock's monument, visitors could see the town of York and the sails and steamers of Lake Ontario. *(Courtesy of the Ontario Archives, ACC 6326 18495)*

the nearby limestone quarries. According to one source, the foundation stone was laid on 1 June 1824 in a ceremony involving Masonic honours. William Lyon Mackenzie, who had recently opened a newspaper office in Queenston, was a prominent figure in that service. He placed a copy of an issue of *The Colonial Advocate* into the cavity of the stone, but it was ordered removed by the lieutenant governor of Upper Canada, Major General Sir Peregrine Maitland, because of Mackenzie's anti-government stance.[20]

Through the summer the bottom portion of the monument housing a tomb to encase the remains of Brock and Macdonell was built. An accident occurred on 28 August when a labourer named Daniel Keith died as the result of a fall at the construction site.[21] Although references to the tower suggest that it was erected in its entirety during that first summer, other evidence exists to show that the work took several years.

With the project well on its way, the first cold days of autumn swept over the Heights and preparations were made for a second, grand funeral and reburial of the fallen heroes.

13 OCTOBER 1824
THE SECOND BURIAL

The grandeur of Brock's first burial was outdone by the ceremony that took place in 1824. Again crowds of civilians, numbering 8,000 according to one authority, gathered to witness the spectacle at Fort George, Queenston and along the road that joined them. Everyone turned out in their finery, but the most striking outfits proved to be the Highland costumes worn by Donald and Duncan Macdonell, brothers of the general's aide. Also, attracting much attention were John Brant and the other chiefs from the Six Nations on the Grand River attired in traditional native dress.[22]

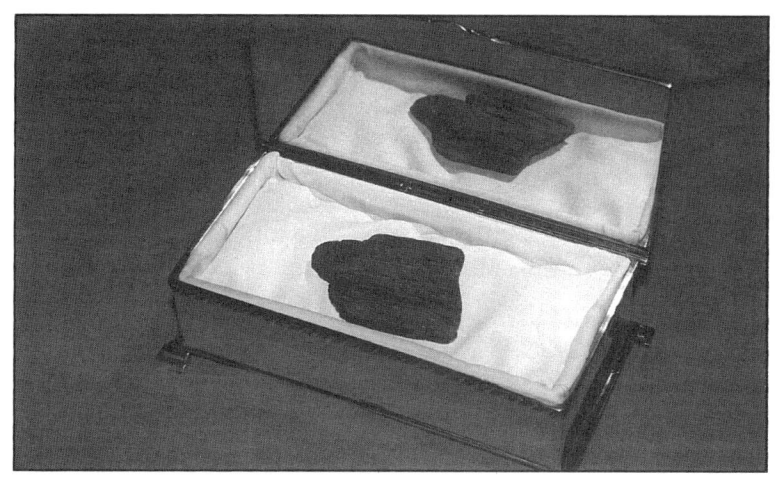

On display at the Lundy's Lane Museum in Niagara Falls is a piece of cedar-like wood that is reputed to have been part of General Brock's first casket.

Colonel James Fitzgibbon, one of Brock's proteges from the 49th Regiment, was among the veterans who attended the second funeral. He wrote: "Nothing, certainly, could exceed the interest manifested by the people of the Province upon this occasion; and numbers from the neighbouring State of New York, by their presence and conduct, proved how highly the Americans revere the memory of our lamented chief."[23]

The First and Fourth Regiments of the Lincoln Militia were called out to line the route to Queenston, standing forty paces apart, as far as their numbers would allow.[24] A large army wagon had been converted into a hearse. It was covered with black cloth, driven by a black coachman and drawn by four black horses each handled by a black groom.

Prior to this time, and in circumstances veiled in secrecy, the bodies of Brock and Macdonell had been disinterred and placed in new caskets. One source quoted this observation: "Although twelve years had elapsed since the interment, the body of the General had undergone little change, his features being nearly perfect, and easily recognized, while that of Lieutenant-Colonel Macdonell was a mass of decomposition."[25] Later, Brock's original coffin was been blown up, so that pieces of it could be distributed among officers in the armed services; one such shard is on display in the Lundy's Lane Museum in Niagara Falls.

When the caskets were placed on the hearse, an attendant climbed onto the wagon and secured a large cocked hat to the coffin containing Brock's remains. The general had ordered the new hat, adorned with ostrich feathers, from England as part of the change in uniform he was required to make in 1811 when he was advanced to the rank of major general. It did not arrive in Canada until after he had died and was passed along to Captain James Brock of the 49th Regiment, a cousin of the general. Captain Brock later presented the hat to George Ball, a miller living near Niagara. The Ball family offered to lend the hat to the organizers of the funeral who readily accepted the contribution and gave it a place of prominence. It attracted much attention, and when the formal ceremony was over, many onlookers were eager to examine the hat and to try it on.[26]

About 10:00 a. m. on that Wednesday morning the funeral car was led through the gate of Fort George by a single officer from the military staff, followed by a company of Grenadiers, a band intoning its sombre strains and a unit of the 76th Regiment. As the hearse reached the gate a salute of nineteen guns was fired. Behind the hearse strode Commissioners Dickson and Clark (Nichol had died), governmental administrators, judges, members of the executive council and His Excellency, Lieutenant Governor Sir Peregrine Maitland. A second wing of the 76th and sundry militia officers trailed the procession, which had turned up the road to Queenston at a slow pace. As the end of the parade passed each Lincoln militiaman, he wheeled inward to join the march.

When the head of the column had reached an appropriate distance from the fort, a brief pause was ordered. The dignitaries climbed into carriages and the caravan resumed

When he was promoted to the rank of major general in 1811, Isaac Brock ordered a new hat, complete with an ostrich feather fringe, from England. The hat was obtained by the Niagara Historical Society in 1896.

its journey at a faster rate. It took three hours for it to make the ten kilometre (seven mile) journey to Queenston. Along the way the local populace came out to pay respect to the fallen heroes and then join the train.

As it approached Queenston it was greeted by a second long file, formed by militiamen from the Second and Third Lincoln Regiments. When the procession reached the foot of the escarpment, another halt was made while the entire assembly stood in silence for several minutes within sight of the place where Isaac Brock had been slain. Apparently, that spot had been marked, although no such marker survived to later years. Then the march continued slowly up the Portage Road, past the redan battery and toward the site where the base of the tower had been constructed.

The dignitaries alighted from their carriages, took their place in line, and the funeral car was drawn toward the mausoleum. The spectators closed around to view the removal of the caskets from the hearse. Before the eyes of thousands, the pall bearers carried the heroes to the vault and deposited them into two stone sepulchres. Unfortunately, the actual appearance of the tomb and the foundation of the tower was not recorded by any of the numerous eyewitnesses. Later events suggested, however, that the coffins of Brock and Macdonell were lowered into a single vault below ground level and covered by stone slabs.

As the general and his friend were laid to rest for the second time, the regiments presented arms and an artillery battery on the Heights fired a salute of nineteen guns. No official addresses appear to have been made by the dignitaries, although it seems likely that wreathes and memorial displays were placed on the tomb. When these tributes had been made, the ceremony was officially closed by a march of the assembled military units around the site. After that everyone departed from the Heights.

In the spring of 1825 Francis Hall renewed work on the tower. The project continued through the summer and into the fall, and was resumed the following year. Thomas Dickson died in 1825, leaving Thomas Clark as the sole surviving commissioner. He sought the money that would be needed to see the project through to its end, but subscriptions were slow in coming. By mid-1827 the tower had been raised to a suitable height, but the inscription intended for its base had not been finished. The fence around the observation deck was not in place and a start had yet to be made on the statue of the general, originally planned to be placed on the tower's summit.

It appears that Brock's tower was never completed to the prescribed design. No mention can be found in any of the newspapers of the day regarding a special ceremony to commemorate the culmination of the project. In January of 1840 (three years after Thomas Clark's death) a new committee was formed to investigate the state of the account set up to build the structure.[27] The commissioners discovered that an additional grant of £600 had been voted from the provincial coffers, but there was no evidence that it had been spent. They also revealed that concern had been raised about the appearance of the tower and its unfinished state. Francis Hall had submitted an estimate of the cost of completing the work, but, again, there was no proof that Hall's suggestions were followed.

Brock's first monument, finished or not, was the grandest memorial in British North America. It stood 41 metres (135 feet) tall. A base had been built over the tomb, measuring about six metres (20 feet) square and six metres high. A column in Tuscan style rose above the base, having at its summit a pedestal upon which a simple ornament, rather than a statue of Brock, was placed. A staircase spiralled up through the three metre (10 feet) wide core of the column, which opened onto an observation deck just below the summit.

An inscription was mounted over the entrance. It noted that the provincial legislature had dedicated the monument to Brock's memory and his valiant civil service. The inscription

For a decade and a half Brock's first tower stood on Queenston Heights, unequalled by any other frontier memorial. *(Courtesy of the National Archives of Canada, C9347)*

closed with the following:

> *He fell in action the 13th day of October 1812, in the 43rd year of his age. Honoured and beloved by the people whom he governed, and deplored by his Sovereign to whose service his life had been devoted. His remains are deposited in this vault, as also those of his aide de camp, Lieutenant-colonel John Macdonell, who died of his wounds, the 14th of October 1812, received the day before in action.*[28]

Brock's monument became a destination for the small number of people who toured North America in the 1820s and 1830s. One such visitor was Harriet Martineau who, in 1838, published a book about her travels entitled *Retrospect of Western Travel*. When Martineau and her companions reached the summit above Queenston they encountered "the portress, an active little Irishwoman, waiting to let us in. . . . She and her husband have, for showing the monument, sixty dollars a season."[29]

The view from the observation deck was impressive. Martineau wrote: "To the left a prodigious sweep of forest terminates in blue Canadian hills. On the right is the American shore, at this time gaudy with autumn woods. There stands Lewiston . . . at our feet lay Queenston . . . The green river rushes between its lofty wooded banks . . . , with three or four bends, to the lake."[30] The Irish custodian of the tower, at whose cottage Martineau dined, regretted that she did not have a telescope for the use of the visitors. There had been one, but she claimed that a party of Americans had thrown it down from the top of the tower and then refused to compensate her for its loss.

THE EXPLOSION

The single most spectacular event in the brief history of General Brock's first monument at Queenston occurred during the predawn hours of Good Friday, 17 April 1840. At 4:00 a.m. that day an explosion shook the tower and startled the residents of Queenston from their sleep.

Villagers rushed out of their homes and saw at once a vast, white cloud of smoke rising against the dark sky above the Heights. Some of them hurried up the slope to inspect the scene and were shocked to discover that Brock's monument had been severely damaged by a charge apparently set at the base of its staircase. "The pedestal was cracked on one side," noted one newspaper correspondent, "the shaft of the column was extensively cracked in several places, and that portion of the column, above the gallery, was dreadfully shattered. The wooden staircase, inside, was blown into a mass of ruins."[31]

Closer examination of the tower led some observers to conclude that if the door at the top of the stairway had been tightly closed, the tower would have fallen. A public meeting was held on 17 June at the Queenston Hotel to discuss various courses of action. Francis Hall attended the session and proposed that the monument could be repaired with cement and new stone at a cost of about £370. This opinion was sharply criticized by others who proclaimed that the damaged monument should be pulled down and replaced by a structure that would reflect the public's admiration for Brock and indignation for the vandalism that had marred his memorial.[32]

Shortly after the tower was vandalized Lieutenant Governor Sir George Arthur offered a £1000 reward for the capture of the individuals responsible for the act, but no one was ever taken into custody. An investigation was launched by authorities on both sides of the river, which led quickly to the speculation that a fellow named Benjamin Lett had masterminded the deed. Lett was an Irish-Canadian who had been involved in some of the rebellious activity during 1837 and after.[33] It was said that a relative of his had been killed when government troops stormed Navy Island and sent the steamer *Caroline* over Niagara Falls in flames. With revenge added to his anti-British politics, Lett allegedly vowed to get retribution.

Although he was not apprehended in Upper Canada, Benjamin Lett found himself behind bars in New York State shortly after the near-destruction of Brock's Monument. His imprisonment was in connection with the detonation of a bomb aboard the steamer *Great Britain* while it was lying at Oswego taking on passengers for Lewiston. Fortunately, the device had been set improperly, and apart from exploding with a loud report and burning one man severely, it managed only to produce lots of smoke and pandemonium.

A quick investigation led to the arrest of Lett where he was staying at the United States Hotel in Oswego, armed with four pistols and a Bowie knife. An accomplice of his, named Dafoe, admitted to having participated in the crime and described the bomb that he and Lett had assembled. They had packed a steamer trunk with inflammable material wrapped around two jugs containing inflammables including turpentine, white rosin, shellac and saltpetre. Gunpowder was put into a third jar, which was placed beneath the other two, and fitted with a fuse that was passed through a hole in the trunk so that it could be lit. In the same manner, perhaps, as they had planted the bomb at Queenston, Lett and Dafoe delivered the trunk to the *Great Britain*, lit the fuse and departed, quickly.[34]

Benjamin Lett was tried before a jury at Oswego on 22 June 1840. Pleading innocence, he "maintained a dogged and hardened composure during the whole trial and occasionally put on a sneering smile."[35] The case was presented quickly and the jury wasted little time in making its decision. Lett was found guilty of arson in the fourth degree and sentenced immediately to seven years at the penitentiary at Auburn, New York. As things turned out, however, he did not serve his term.

While he was being taken by train to the penitentiary on the night of 26 June, Benjamin Lett managed to escape from a

S.E. View of "Brock's Monument" on Queenston Heights as it appeared May 9th A.D. 1841.

(Courtesy of the Ontario Archives, ACC U579 S 12404.)

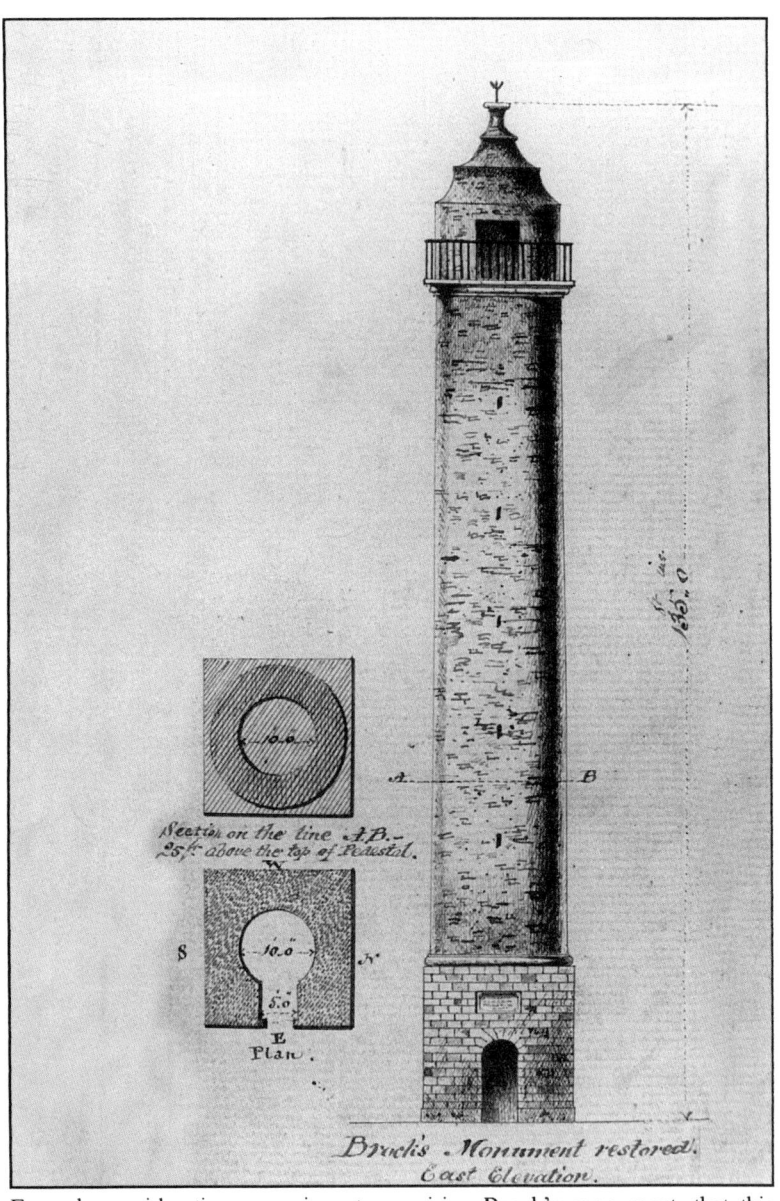

Enough consideration was given to repairing Brock's monument, that this plan was made. The identity of the draftsman is uncertain. *(Courtesy of the Ontario Archives, ACC 4579)*

deputy named Erie Poor, who had been assigned to guard him and other prisoners. Although he was shackled, Lett succeeded in bolting from his seat, evading the grasp of the deputy and leaping from the train as it bumped along at the speed of 20 miles per hour. Deputy Poor was later accused of not making an adequate effort to track down Lett, even though the convict left a trail of blood and was thought to have been badly injured. Rewards were posted, but Lett made a clean escape.

Within a short time Benjamin Lett came to public attention again. On 2 July 1840 a notice appeared in Rochester warning people not to sail on one of the two cruises the steamer *Gore* would take as part of the Fourth of July celebrations. The announcement was signed by "Benjamin Lett, P. C. On board the flag Ship *Revenge*, off the Ducks."[36] It proved to be an empty threat since nothing unpleasant happened to the *Gore*. Lett was eventually arrested in Buffalo and sent to prison for four years. On his release, he went west and died in 1858 in Milwaukee.[37]

30 JULY 1840
THE GREAT PUBLIC MEETING

The attack on Brock's monument produced such a cry of outrage among the public that Lieutenant Governor Arthur announced that an open air meeting would be held on the Heights above Queenston to discuss the matter. When Thursday, 30 July was picked as the day for the event, thousands of people made their plans to travel to Queenston. So great was the interest in the meeting, that the thirtieth was proclaimed a public holiday in Toronto, Niagara, Queenston, St. Catharines and elsewhere.[38]

In preparation for the great assembly, a large platform was constructed near the damaged tower. On either side of the platform "spacious wooden tents" were erected with seating for the ladies in attendance, and, at the bottom of the slope, a large pavilion was raised where a banquet could be held after the proceedings. Apart from these official preparations, many people arrived at Queenston before the thirtieth and set up their tents on and around the Heights, giving it the appearance of a military camp.

The crowds swelled to eight thousand when 30 July dawned clear and fair. Those people who had claimed their space on the Heights were treated to one of the first spectacles of the day. The smoke trails of a fleet of steamers came into view on Lake Ontario, nine of them in all, five from Toronto, two from Cobourg and Kingston, and two from the Hamilton area. HMS *Traveller*, carrying the Lieutenant Governor and his staff, led the way up the river at about 10:00 a. m. The ships created an impressive sight, all of them being festooned with patriotic banners and packed with exuberant passengers.

A military guard provided by the Queen's Dragoons and militia units greeted Lieutenant Governor Arthur who had brought along the band of the 93rd Regiment, resplendent in its traditional Highlander regalia. Accompanied by the strains of "Old England," the official party got into carriages and proceeded up the winding road to the summit of the escarpment. As they reached the meeting place, an artillery battery boomed out a salute to the dignitaries and the sanctity of the occasion.

At 1:00 p. m. Sir George, dressed in the uniform of a major general, convened the meeting. Before him stood and sat thousands of spectators, including "Many an old uniform, which of old, bore the brunt of years of war . . . [worn by] some grey veteran, who stepped firm and erect 'beneath the burden of four score . . .'"[39] Above them all flapped a large Union Jack, fastened to the lightning rod of the tower by a daring, young sailor from the *Traveller* who had climbed the damaged structure.

Sir George opened the proceedings with a speech extolling the virtues of Isaac Brock and decrying the villainy of the felons' act. The assembly responded to him with tumultuous applause and then settled down again to listen to no fewer than twenty-four more speakers. Typical of the orations were the comments of the Chief Justice of Upper Canada, Sir John Beverley Robinson. He spoke effectively, recalling the fateful day in 1812:

Among the many who are assembled here from all parts of this Province, I know there are some who saw as I did, with grief, the body of the lamented general borne from the field on which he fell . . . They can never, I am sure, forget the countenances of that gallant regiment which he had long commanded, when they saw deposited in the earth, the lamented officer, who had been for many years their pride.

If it were intended by those who committed this shameful outrage, that the injury should be irreparable, the scene which is now before us, on these interesting heights, shows that they little understood the feelings of veneration for the memory of Brock which still dwells in the hearts of the people of Upper Canada.[40]

Eleven resolutions were presented by the various speakers. Each orator called for an affirmation of one of the convictions that had prompted the public's emotion: that Brock was still greatly revered; that the bombing of the monument was a malicious and traitorous act; that a new memorial be raised as soon as possible; and, that a committee be formed to steer the project. The crowd responded with loud support to every proposal. The last of the resolutions invited a public recognition of the personal donations already made by Charles Poulet Thomson, the Governor General of British North America, and by the Lieutenant Governor of New Brunswick, Sir Richard Jackson, and the Commander-in-Chief of the forces in British North America, Sir John Harvey. Adjournment came shortly after acceptance of the eleventh resolution.

Following the meeting, Sir George Arthur and about 600 of the most influential people present withdrew to the pavilion at the base of the hill for a banquet. The Lieutenant Governor and his staff ate at a table said to be the one used by Lieutenant Governor Simcoe in the 1790s, purchased by the Woodruff family after Simcoe's departure. More speeches and many toasts interrupted the dinner, so that it lasted into the evening. At sunset Arthur left Queenston on the *Traveller*, while the thousands who had enjoyed the festivities retired to their tents or trudged homeward.

THE SECOND TOWER

At least twenty different men served on the new Brock Monument committee during its existence. They were led by Sir Allan Napier McNab. A loyal supporter of Tory policies, he was a natural choice as president of the committee established to replace Brock's memorial. As a fifteen-year-old, McNab had been a member of the advance guard that captured Fort Niagara in December 1813. He later became a lawyer and politician and was knighted for his role in suppressing the Rebellion of 1837 in Upper Canada. McNab was joined on the committee by other firm loyalists, including John Macauley, the Inspector General of Upper Canada, John Beverley Robinson, the prominent justice official, and William Hamilton Merritt, one of the province's most industrious businessmen and politicians.

In 1842, after meeting to establish their ground rules and to advertise for public subscriptions, the commissioners initiated a contest for a design for the monument. Architects and engineers, amateur and professional, were quick to respond, submitting thirty-five plans in total. An Egyptian-style obelisk, with neither inner stairway nor observation space, designed by Thomas Young of Toronto, was selected as the best one and presented with the prize of £25.[41]

Unlike arrangements made to build the original monument, there were no funds allocated by the provincial

Thomas Young's design for the new monument was for a more formidable structure than the earlier tower. Completion of the work was expected in 1844, but funding fell short. *(Courtesy of the Metropolitan Toronto Reference Library, T30317)*

government for the new project. It was intended that donations would cover the costs, and reasonable success was achieved by September 1842, when the committee reported that more than £3200 had been collected. Private citizens had contributed a portion of the sum, as had a group representing the citizens of Montreal. The officers and men of the militia of Canada West (formerly Upper Canada) and New Brunswick were recognized for their subscriptions. Special notice was made also of the amounts raised by numerous communities of the Chippawa, Huron, Wyandot, Moravian, Munsee, Oneida, Mississauga and Mohawk tribes.[42]

The estimated cost of erecting Young's monument was £5,000, so McNab and his fellow commissioners decided to appeal to the Governor General of British North America for his assistance. On 30 September 1842, they presented a petition to Sir Charles Bagot at Government House in Kingston requesting that he advise the legislature of the province of Canada to supplement the fund.[43] Bagot agreed to approach the legislative leaders, but they were distracted by other financial needs. Without sufficient money to build the monument, Young's winning design languished through the 1840s and was all but forgotten as the next decade dawned.

The mission of the Brock Monument committee gained fresh momentum in 1852. Contributions and accrued interest had raised the assets to £5794.[44] The fact that a design had already been chosen for the tower was ignored by the commissioners when they decided in June of that year to offer a prize of £25 to the winner of a new contest. Several representatives of the committee met at Queenston on 2 August to receive submissions, and were disappointed to find designs being offered by only six individuals. The small number was said to be due to a boycott of the contest by architects involved in the first competition, the results of which they believed had been rudely ignored.

Despite the fact that his earlier winning plan had been rejected by the committee, Thomas Young proposed another monument, "a Grecian Doric column, chaste and affective in

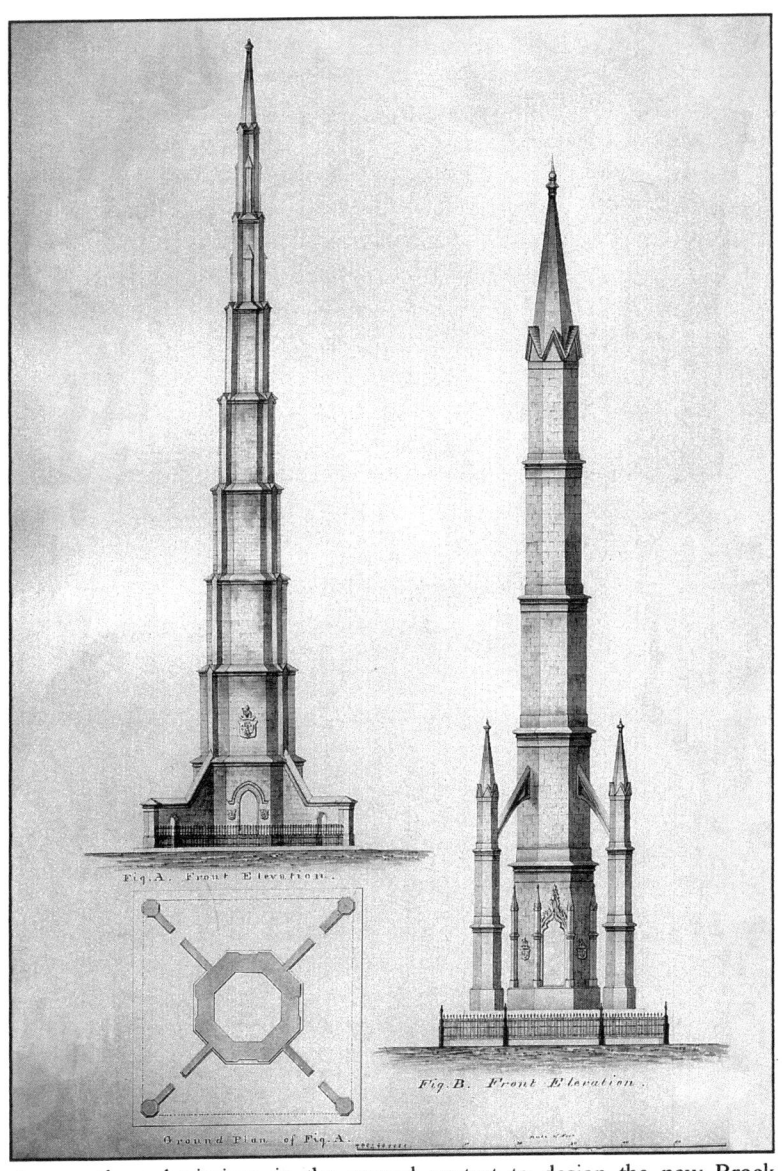

Among the submissions in the second contest to design the new Brock monument was this plan, by an unknown architect, featuring optional versions of "a Gothic Cross." *(Courtesy of the Metropolitan Toronto Reference Library, Howard Papers, 483)*

character."[45] Young's idea was rejected, however, as were the designs of four other men, one of which was described by a critic as "a Gothic Mausoleum of most wretched character and miserably rendered."[46]

The submissions from William Thomas were given special attention. Thomas had set up his architectural office in Toronto in 1843 after immigrating from England and had rapidly become one of the foremost designers in British North America. He had been responsible for numerous public buildings like the court house in the town of Niagara built in 1847.[47] During his career he also created the designs for larger structures like St. Lawrence Hall and St. Michael's Cathedral in Toronto.

For the Brock contest Thomas submitted two proposals. One showed an archway upon which was a statue of Brock riding his horse into battle. Thomas' second scheme, for a lofty tower on a high pedestal, was initially considered too delicately decorated, but, at a meeting of the full committee on 10 August 1852 in Toronto, it was chosen as the best of the bunch.

Details about the proposed monument were published

The lowest visible portion of the monument is the sub-basement. Upon it is built a pedestal, intended to raise the overall height of the tower. The decorations feature sculpted lions and depictions of Brock's achievements. The fluted column rises to the capital and the wings of Victory.

in the *Canadian Journal* in September 1852 and showed how the original plan differed in some aspects from the tower that was eventually built.[48]

The base of the monument, identified as the sub-basement, was to be erected on a raised platform, or foundation. Thomas' conception of the foundation was not described in the *Journal* article, but it was later revealed that it was 12.5 metres (40 feet) square and 3.1 metres (10 feet) thick and made of large stone blocks. Into this foundation were cut two tombs containing stone sarcophagi into which the caskets of Brock and Macdonell would be placed.[49]

The sub-basement was to be eight metres (27 feet) tall and 11.5 metres (38 feet) square. Externally, it would have a solid and plain appearance, except for one side, upon which would be affixed an inscription in bronze letters memorializing the general. A door on the south side would provide access to a corridor wrapping around the staircase and two vaults to the east and west of it. Light would be transmitted to the interior by a series of round openings, decorated with wreaths. A sculpted lion was to stand on each of the upper corners of the base, proudly holding a shield bearing Brock's coat of arms. Around the sub-basement would be erected a "dwarf-wall," 24 metres (77 feet) square, with sculpted military trophies, six metres (20 feet) tall, on each corner.

A pedestal would be built atop the sub-basement, primarily as a means of elevating the column above the trees that surrounded the site. It was to be about 4.8 metres (16 feet, 9 inches) square and eleven and a half metres (38 feet) tall. Each side of the pedestal would feature bas reliefs depicting Brock's achievements and his coat of arms.

On the pedestal would be placed a cap, or die, with more wreathed openings meant to illuminate the inside. The column was described as being of the "Roman Composite Order." It was to be composed of segments, forming a fluted shaft, 3.1 metres (10 feet) in diameter and twenty-nine metres (95 feet) tall.

At the summit of the column would sit the capital. This

The capital sits on the top of the column. Four sculptures of Victory spreading her wings stand around the capital between other ornate decorations. William Thomas' original plan was to have an external observation deck on the abacus, which is the top surface of the capital. An enclosed observation post is in the cippus, above which stands the statue of Brock.

platform would be 3.8 metres (12 feet, six inches) high and feature a sculpture of winged Victory on each face. The wing tips of the Victories would meet at the corners above military shields, helmets and the fierce images of lions. The idea for the details of the capital apparently came from an ancient column located near Rome. The upper part of the capital, known as the abacus, would be 4.5 metres (15 feet) square, enough space "for persons to stand outside to view the surrounding scenery." William Thomas also intended that the ornamentation on the upper portion of the abacus would make it possible "to avoid the unsightly appearance of iron railings."[50]

An enclosed observation deck was also to be provided for sightseers. This was the cippus, a cylindrical chamber at the tops of the staircase, measuring 1.9 metres (6 feet) in diameter and made from galvanized, cast iron, with wreathed portals for observations. On the cippus a statue of Isaac Brock would stand 4.8 metres (16 feet) tall.

The entire structure was to be fashioned of Queenston limestone, including the staircase which would feature 250 steps. The plume of Brock's hat would be 57 metres (185 feet) above the ground, making the monument the second tallest structure of its kind in the world. Only Sir Christopher Wren's column erected to commemorate the great fire of London in 1666 (62 metres, 202 feet) would exceed it. Taller than any of the columns raised to honour Lord Nelson and Napoleon, William Thomas' monument to Brock was to become a symbol of British patriotism in the frontier province of Canada.

JULY 1853
THE THIRD BURIAL

Contractual matters and other arrangements for the building of the new monument were settled during the first half of 1853. William Thomas was to oversee the project, while John Worthington would supervise the daily work of the labourers. Stone carvers David Cochrane and Robert Pollock were hired to effect the many ornaments of the structure.

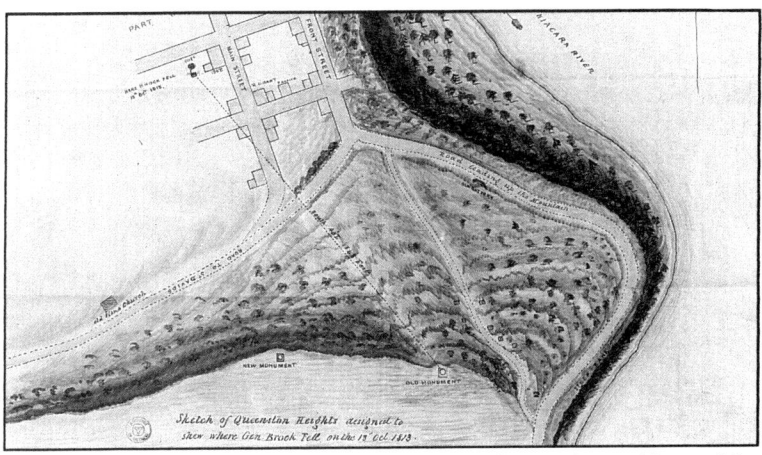

This view, drawn in 1860 by George Keefer, indicates the positions of the first and second monuments. Notable also is a commonly made error about the date of the battle. *(Courtesy of the Ontario Archives, MV 1626, 11)*

Work at Queenston Heights began in July with cleaning up the area around the old monument and preparing the ground for the new site, located about one hundred metres to the west on the loftiest point on the Heights. Although it had been predicted that the column of the 1820s would tumble to the ground soon after it had been vandalized, that tower, somewhat ravaged by time and neglect, still stood. Its builder, Francis Hall, had claimed in 1840 that the damage inflicted by the bomb could be repaired, and his edifice proved him right. It took several blasts of explosives before the tower was finally levelled on Saturday, 9 July.[51]

With Hall's monument reduced to rubble and cleared away, the next task was to remove the remains of General Brock and Lieutenant Colonel Macdonell from their tombs and to reinter them in temporary graves. Unfortunately, a lack of foresight on the part of the monument committee, the architect and contractor turned this procedure into a controversy. No effort was made to conduct a ceremony equal to the solemnity of the occasion, nor was a public announcement of the disinterment of the heroes made. Nevertheless, a group of curious citizens was present when the labourers undertook their grisly task with an apparent lack of decorum. Several days later a letter of protest appeared in the *Niagara Chronicle*, signed simply by "Loyalists." They lambasted William Thomas for failing to show the remains of Brock and Macdonell the respect they deserved.

In his own letter to the *Chronicle* Thomas rebutted his critics by explaining the propriety of his actions:

I took the two shells from Toronto on the day appointed and very carefully had the vault opened and placed all the remains and fragments of the broken coffins in each separate shell and fastened the original silver plates, with the inscriptions engraved thereon and accompanied them to the burial ground [on the Hamilton estate in Queenston] *where I had them placed in a grave eight feet deep as proper security.*[52]

The small cemetery at the west end of the Hamilton estate in Queenston was the third resting place of Isaac Brock and John Macdonell.

Another version of the incident was printed in *The Niagara Mail*, describing in more detail the scene at the monument. Eyewitnesses informed the *Mail's* correspondent that the tombs of the heroes had been damaged by the explosion in 1840, and, presumably, by the final destruction of the column. "The remains of the illustrious pair," observed the writer, "consisting of their bones, the skulls quite entire, and dust were much mixed with the fragments of lime and stone which had once formed their tomb." Two boxes made of unfinished pine planks were brought forward and "the clownish and ignorant workmen proceeded, without ceremony to *shovel* up the bones, dust and dirt, all together."[53] Either William Thomas or an indignant onlooker stepped in at that point to tell the labourers whose bones they were tossing around, after which more care was taken. When the tomb had been cleared, the coffins were loaded on a wagon and carted down the escarpment to the Hamilton estate. The date of the reburial is uncertain, although it seems likely to have taken place during the week of 11 July.

13 OCTOBER 1853
THE FOURTH BURIAL

While the remains of Brock and Macdonell lay in the quiet burial ground in the village of Queenston through the summer of 1853, work pressed forward to prepare the sub-basement and tombs of the new monument. Plans were made by a subcommittee chaired by William Hamilton Merritt for another grand ceremony to honour the heroes of 1812, but these arrangements were apparently not made until late in September. Thursday, 13 October was selected as the appropriate date for the service and notices were published in newspapers to alert the public.[54]

Around 8:00 a.m. on the forty-first anniversary of the battle of Queenston Heights carriages and wagons began to crowd the roads leading to Queenston. The weather was clear and pleasant, the whole area being tinged with the gold of autumnal leaves. Offices and workshops were closed so that labourers could attend the event. Throughout the towns and villages flags were raised to half mast in honour of the fallen heroes. Atop the Heights three tall flagstaffs wore Union Jacks at their peaks.

Aged veterans made their appearance in their militia uniforms. John C. Ball, who had been with the militia artillery at the battle, was present in company with Captain Brown and his detachment of the Hamilton Independent Artillery. The old colonels, Kirby and Servos, who had participated in the capture of Fort Niagara, waited to take their parts as official pall bearers. Representatives of the aboriginal nations also were on hand. Chief John S. Johnson of the Six Nation Mohawks, the grandson of Joseph Brant, was there, attired "in full war costume with scalping knife and tomahawk."[55] Some of the old-timers who had gone to their graves were remembered with displays of black crepe. One widow in Queenston had a line strung above the street from her house, from which she hung two union jacks, bracketed in mourning cloth.

Steamships arrived from across the lake, bringing dignitaries and common people to Queenston. The Lieutenant Governor of the province of Canada was not among the official party travelling from Kingston. In his place Colonel Donald Macdonell, Deputy Adjutant General of Militia for Canada West, and brother of Brock's aide, led the delegation. From Canada East came Lieutenant Colonel De Salaberry, Deputy Adjutant General for Canada East, and son of the De Salaberry who had defeated the Americans at Chateauguay in October 1813. With them travelled Colonel Étienne-Paschal Taché, one of the most prominent politicians and governmental ministers in Canada East. Sir Allan McNab was also absent, his duties as president of the monument committee having been assumed by William Hamilton Merritt.

Around 11:00 a. m. the official procession began to assemble on King Street. The imposing funeral car impressed everyone who saw it and gave great credit to William Thomas, its designer. The huge wagon had been fitted with three, tiered platforms, rising almost four metres (12 feet) above the ground, with pillars that rose even higher on the corners. It was covered with black cloth and decorated with Brock's and Macdonell's coats of arms. On each side were "military trophies," comprising muskets, swords and bayonets used during the war. Union Jacks were draped on the corners, while the British colours were arranged in mourning bands across the centre. Six black horses were harnessed to the wagon, each of them festooned with ornaments and Brock's arms.

Apparently, a party of labourers had been busy at the Hamilton estate since early in the morning, unearthing once again the remains of Brock and Macdonell. A transfer of the remains into new caskets is likely to have been made at or near the cemetery. The silver plates that had identified the bodies since 1812 were also affixed to the new coffins. These preparations were complete before the procession on King Street was put in its proper order, so the caskets were put down in the laneway that ran from the graveyard to the street. Bystanders were silenced when Colonel Macdonell suddenly appeared, walking up the lane to stand by the coffins. After several minutes of quiet contemplation, Macdonell returned to the street, "wiping tears from his manly cheek."[56]

Another insightful observation was made about the new, wooden caskets that had been provided. A correspondent for *The Mail* wrote: "they ought to have been of the full size of the men whose ashes were to be laid in them. They were not over five feet in length we are told and a future generation examining them, might conclude that Brock was a mere pigmy in stature, whereas, both he and Mcdonell were quite large and tall men."[57]

It was not until 2:00 p. m. that the procession finally got underway. Led by the Canadian Rifle Regiment and its band, and trailed by mourners, veterans, commissioners and dignitaries, the funeral car advanced slowly up the road toward the escarpment. The caskets were positioned at a height that made them visible to all onlookers. Atop Brock's coffin was fastened the cocked hat lent by the Ball family during the reburial in 1824. From the village "the sight was very imposing. The brow and side of the lofty hill were covered with people; and the artillery fired minute guns as the cortege approached."[58] Estimations of the number of people in attendance ranged between 12,000 and 15,000.

The press of people around the base of the monument delayed the arrival of the hearse. At length, the caskets were taken down and deposited in their separate vaults, Brock to the north and Macdonell to the south; the architect's original plans had been altered so that the entrance was shifted to face eastward.

Next, Colonel Macdonell applied the mortar, with assistance from Lieutenant Colonel De Salaberry, that would cement the corner stone in place. Macdonell was then presented with a silver trowel bearing an inscription on one side and Brock's coat of arms and the number of the 49th Regiment encircled by a wreath, on the reverse side. Above the tombs the colours of the militia regiments were unfurled.

William Hamilton Merritt (1793-1862) was the renowned businessman who promoted the development of inland navigation, railways and bridges. His position as one of the leading citizens of Canada West led to his appointment to the Brock Monument committee. *(Courtesy of the National Archives of Canada, C29891)*

Walter Dickson stood at the podium on the platform erected adjacent to the monument to read from a parchment containing a brief review of Brock's death, the interment in the first monument, the attack on that structure and the laying of the new foundation stone. When Dickson had finished his recitation, the parchment, along with several other papers and coins, was placed in the foundation stone. The stone was then lowered into place as the artillery and the riflemen fired three volleys.

William Hamilton Merritt stepped to centre stage at that point and delivered a lengthy address. Merritt reviewed the history of the war, emphasizing Brock's part in it, and also described several other engagements and their significance. He began his speech with an apology for not having been able to find a more distinguished speaker to perform the task, as the building committee had requested. Merritt's presentation was not especially successful, for it appears either that he was uneasy about speaking to such a large assembly, or that his oratorical talents were not equal to the occasion. The correspondent for *The Mail* noted: "Mr. Merritt spoke under some embarrassment being, evidently, deeply affected by the imposing sight of so many of his old companions in arms around him or the reminiscences of the past."[59] To make matters worse, some of the veterans on the podium interrupted the speech to point out their versions of events and when they happened, making the task all that much more difficult for Merritt.

When Merritt returned to his seat, no doubt relieved to have fulfilled his responsibility, David Thorburn spoke to the crowd about the role played by the Indians during the 1812 War and read a decree from Chief John Johnson. This was followed by an eloquent commentary from Colonel Taché, who recounted the tale of war events in Lower Canada. He concluded his remarks by proposing that monuments be erected throughout the country to commemorate the decisive engagements of the war. Colonel Clarke rose to second the motion, after which Colonel Kirby presented a short talk about the war and made a second recommendation that subscriptions be commenced across the province to fund the building of the monuments.

Those were the final comments of the program, except for a call for three times three cheers for Queen Victoria. The sun by that time was near the western horizon and, as the crowd slowly dispersed and the elements of the procession withdrew, the dignitaries went down to Mr. Wynn's Hotel in Queenston. There, and in all the local taverns, "the stout old soldiers fought their battles over again until a late hour. Thus ended one of the most interesting days ever witnessed in Upper Canada."[60]

RAISING THE SECOND TOWER

In the spring of 1854 work on the tower moved forward, but not without some problems. John Worthington revealed to William Thomas that he was having difficulties in

The celebrations at Brock's Monument drew crowds of people who marvelled at William Thomas' magnificent structure. *(Courtesy of the National Archives of Canada, C58782)*

getting sufficient quantities of stone. By mid-March he was ready to lay the blocks that would form the plinth, but only had enough stone to complete one half of the first course in that part of the structure. Thomas wrote to the committee recommending that Worthington be allowed to open a quarry several hundred metres west of the site on the edge of the escarpment.[61]

Sufficient materials were obtained eventually to allow

the project to progress. Workmen crowded over the massive complex of wooden scaffolding that rose around the structure. Huge pieces of stone, some of them weighing three tons, were hoisted into place without any serious loss of time due to accident or injury. By October 1855 Worthington's crews had completed the plinth, raised the column, added the capital and placed the statue of Brock on the summit. During the spring of the next year the lions were put on the corners of the sub-basement, and the enclosure wall and trophies were built. Within a few months the bas-relief depiction of the battle at Queenston, created by Cochrane and Pollock, was inserted into its place on the north face of the plinth.[62]

The building committee reported in October 1857 that the monument, except for a little painting, was complete. Some modifications had been made in William Thomas's original plans. The entire structure had been rotated ninety degrees so that the doorway opened to the east, with the tombs on the north and south. Fifteen fewer than the prescribed 250 steps spiralled up to the observation deck. A small hatchway had been built into the cippus/observation platform, but the upper portion of the capital, the abacus, was not built to have the features that Thomas had intended. As a result, there was not sufficient space for an external observation area, although access to the outside was possible through the hatchway. The inscription on the plinth had been raised in stone rather than bronze as originally planned.

The final phase of work on the new monument involved the landscaping of the surrounding area. The provincial legislature granted the money necessary for this task and architect Thomas was awarded the contract. During 1858, apparently, the landscaping was done. Forty acres of property were cleared and fenced. Additional trees were planted, a large and impressive gateway was erected near the old portage road, and an avenue for carriages was constructed leading up to and around the tower in a circle. A stone lodge was also built at the eastern end of the grounds.[63]

13 OCTOBER 1859
THE INAUGURATION

The official inauguration of the new monument to Isaac Brock did not occur until 1859. It was believed generally that the tower had been finished by 1856, and some disappointment was expressed by individuals who watched a couple of Octobers pass without a proper recognition of the memorial.[64] The critics were soon to be placated, for once more a grand public assembly was organized to open the monument.

Again, the thirteenth of October, a Thursday, was selected as the most suitable day for the event and thousands of people put aside their normal labours to attend the proceedings.[65] About 150 people, including dignitaries and representatives from numerous military units, boarded the steamer *Zimmerman* in Toronto at 8:00 a. m. for the trip to Niagara. That journey proved to be an unpleasant one due to the roughness of the lake, and many passengers were felled by nausea. A stop at the town of Niagara delayed the passage so

Sir Allan Napier McNab (1798-1862) was a lawyer, entrepreneur and politician. He was involved in the development of railways and served as premier of the province of Canada between 1854 and 1856. McNab built the 37-room mansion in Hamilton that has become known as Dundurn Castle. (*Courtesy of the National Archives of Canada, C5317*)

that it was not until after noon hour that the steamer finally reached Queenston. The military units disembarked, formed into a procession, marched through the village and up the escarpment, followed by throngs of civilians. In the meantime, the people already on the Heights had claimed seating near the platform erected at the base of the monument. Some had lined up to pay a fee of one shilling to enter the monument and ascend the staircase to the tiny observation deck nearly two hundred feet above the park.

Around 2:00 p. m., the principals were in their designated places and the meeting was called to order. As in the past, a series of speakers addressed the crowd. Sir Allan McNab chaired the proceedings this time and gave the initial speech. Sir Edmund Head, the Governor General of British North America, was not present owing to a recent death in his family. A celebrity was on hand in the person of General Sir William Fenwick Williams, who had gained eminence in 1855 for his actions in the Crimean War; in 1859 he was to be appointed Commander-in-Chief of British forces in British North America. Asked to speak, Williams reluctantly consented and made a few brief, congratulatory comments. Shortly thereafter the call came for three times three cheers for Queen Victoria, a battery of ordnance fired a salute and adjournment was declared.

A banquet was held in a tent raised adjacent to the tower. Before, during and after the meal, many toasts, remarks and cheers were given, with McNab being congratulated for his public service. William Woodruff, an old veteran, presented McNab with a pocket book said to have been given to Isaac Brock by a lady who had stitched his initials into it with silk. As the sun dipped the crowds dispersed, and the *Zimmerman* steamed off to Toronto. Darkness fell on the stone Brock standing resolutely atop his memorial, his hand outstretched toward the north and the land he had defended with his death.

The stone marker erected in 1860 stands at the foot of the Niagara Escarpment below Brock's Monument near the refurbished printery once operated by William Lyon Mackenzie.

ON THIS SPOT, BROCK FELL

The erection of monuments to Isaac Brock was not finished yet, for in 1860 a new initiative was undertaken to place a marker on the spot where Isaac Brock had been killed. The contract for this job also went to William Thomas, one of the final contracts he fulfilled before his death later that fall. He set out to determine the place where Brock received his mortal wound, but soon found himself frustrated by the inability to find someone who would certify a definite location. He approached William Hamilton Merritt and Thomas Street, among others, but could not get confirmation of the location. He did find evidence that a stake had been driven into the ground to mark the spot and that a thorn bush had grown there also, but beyond those clues, Thomas learned nothing definite.[66]

In the end William Thomas was forced to select a spot

While he was trying to determine the place where Brock fell, William Thomas made a sketch of the escarpment below the second monument showing the notable landmarks. Thomas' sketch may be the best indicator of where Brock actually did fall. *(Source: OA, Niagara Historical Collection Series)*

at the very bottom of the escarpment fifty metres (150 feet) or so west of the main street of Queenston. He was under some pressure to lay out the site and build a foundation for the humble marker, for it was expected that a royal visitor would dedicate the monument.

On Wednesday, 19 September 1860, the Prince of Wales (the future King Edward VII), who was making an extended tour of British North America, arrived at Queenston to participate in the induction of the marker. Present also were John Beverley Robinson, William Hamilton Merritt and Donald Macdonell. The Prince made a few remarks, spread mortar over the stone blocks and the corner piece was lowered into place. The next day Thomas' workers returned to complete the job on the last monument placed at Queenston to honour the fallen general.

IN LATER YEARS

Although the 1860s proved to be a dangerous time for British North America and the young country of Canada, no act similar to Lett's act of vandalism was perpetrated against Brock's lofty monument at Queenston. The site became a popular spot for travellers and picnickers alike, but there was no need for the gathering of thousands and the oratory of public figures. In 1869 a small group of veterans of 1812 assembled on the thirteenth of October to recall the long ago battle and to dine at a tavern in the village, probably the final meeting of the aged warriors. After that the years slipped by to the end of the century and beyond, and Brock and Macdonell lay undisturbed in their tombs.

On the one hundredth anniversary of the Battle of Queenston Heights fifteen hundred people met at Brock's monument to honour the general, his aide and the story of their final struggle. The Union Jack that had been unfurled in 1840 atop the damaged, first tower was carried up the stairway to the summit by Miss Helen Merrill who had borrowed the flag from a member of the United Empire Loyalists organization. The British standard was then affixed to the lightning rod on Brock's statue where it fluttered in the breeze above the crowd. More than thirty floral tributes were placed around the foot of the monument on that sunny, Saturday afternoon, 12 October 1912. Representatives from the Channel Islands Society carried another display down the escarpment to the marker that the late King Edward had commemorated in 1860. Three descendants of the Macdonell family were on hand, as was an officer named J. L. Birney whose father, it was reported, had "lifted Brock from his horse when the general was slain while leading his men up the Heights"; such is the way in which myths are perpetuated.[67]

Assemblies varying in size continued to meet for commemorations as the years passed. Picnickers and concert goers formed the largest crowds that spread out on the spacious parkland around the tower. Brock stood steadfastly in stone through the seasons, until a lightning strike during a thunder storm in 1929 snapped off his right arm. An extensive project was then undertaken to restore the weather-ravaged monument and replace the torso of the statue. A portion of the right shoulder of the original statue eventually found its way to the grounds of the university in St. Catharines named for the general.

No other monument of grand scale, eliciting great public celebration, has been erected to memorialize Sir Isaac Brock, although one last modest marker deserves mention.[68] On the wall of a grey, granite building in the town of St. Peter Port, Guernsey is a plaque identifying the structure as the place where Brock was born (the building had lately served as a "Boots" pharmacy.) The plaque simply states the belief that prompted so many people to put so much effort into memorializing the soldier from Guernsey. The raised, bronze letters read: "He saved Canada."

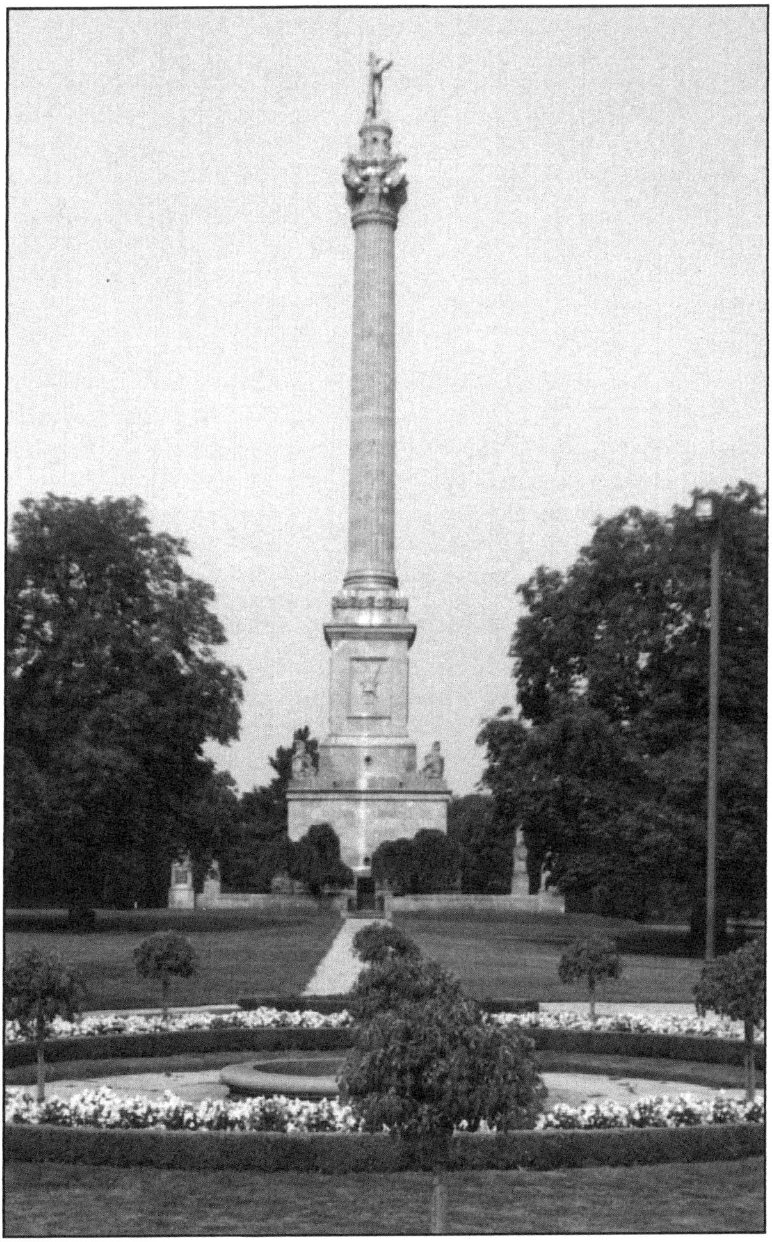

NOTES

1. Walcot narrative, cited in Ludwig Kosche, "Relics of Brock: An Investigation." *Archivaria*, 9, 1979, 33-103, Appendix G, 100-1. Two other Americans claimed to have shot Brock, but, as with Walcot, there is no clear evidence to prove any man's claim, (Appendix H, 102-3).

2. Jarvis narrative, no date, in E. A. Cruikshank, ed. *The Documentary History of the Campaign upon the Niagara Frontier 1812-1814.* 9 vols. (Welland: Lundy's Lane Historical Society, 1896-1908) [hereafter: *DNF*], 4:116.

3. *Ibid.*

4. Funeral Procession described in District General Order by Evans, 16 October 1812, *DNF*, 4:130-1. Details are added to this memo in Benson Lossing, *The Pictorial Field-book of the War of 1812* (New York: Harper and Brothers, 1868), 406.

5. This version of the plate on Brock's coffin was reported in the of 20 October 1853 issue of *The Niagara Mail*. It contains two noticeable errors. Brock was officially knighted on 9 October in England owing to his victory at Detroit, so it would have been impossible for Glegg to know, seven days later, that the honour had been bestowed. Secondly, Brock was born on 6 October 1769, so he was 43 years old at his death. It would seem likely that the correspondent for *The Mail* based his account on inaccurate or inadequate research. There was most definitely a silver plate made to identify Brock's casket, since Glegg referred to it in a letter to Brock's brother, William, 30 December 1813, cited in Kosche, "Relics of Brock...", Appendix B, 79.

6. "[Macdonell's] remains are to be interred to-morrow in the same grave with General Brock." This comment is attributed to Lieutenant McLean of the York Militia, 15 October 1812, *DNF*, 4:115.

7. Cited in *The Daily Globe*, 14 October 1859.

8. Cited in Lossing, *Pictorial Field-book ...*, 406.

9. Speech by Kodeaneyonte, Little Coyote, 6 November 1812, *DNF*, 4:199.

10. "Inventory of furniture, etc. belonging to the estate of Major General Isaac Brock ...", Ontario Archives [hereafter: OA], MU 2143, Miscellaneous Collection, 1812, No. 1. See also "Inventory of General Brock's Effects", *Notes on Niagara 1759-1860, No. 32*, (Niagara: Niagara Historical Society, reprinted 1979), 24-5.

11. Glegg to Brock, 30 December 1813, in Kosche, "Relics of Brock...", Appendix B, 79-80.

12. H. Tupper to Durnford, 10 September 1908, *ibid.*, Appendix C, 97-98. Details about the memorial in *The Daily Globe*, 14 October 1859 and Lossing, *Pictorial Field-book*, 406.

13. Walter Nursey, *The Story of Isaac Brock* (Toronto: McClelland & Stewart, 1923), 218.

14. E. A. Cruikshank, "A Sketch of the Public Life and Services of Robert Nichol...," *Ontario Historical Society Papers and Records*, 19, 1922, 37.

15. Re: "An Act for the erection of a Monument ...", D. B. Read, *Life and Times of Major-General Sir Isaac Brock, K. B.*, (Toronto, W. Briggs, 1894), 252. Nichol to W. Brock, 12 March 1815; W. Brock to Nichol, 8 May 1817; Westmacott to W. Brock, 25 September 1815, National Archives of Canada [hereafter: NAC], Record Group 5, A1, vol. 71:37699-37709.

16. "Report of Commissioners ...," 1 December 1821, *ibid.*:37715-19.

17. 13 January 1824, Clark to Hillier, *ibid.*, 65:34146-8.

18. *Ibid.* Nichol to Hillier, 25 February 1824, *ibid.*:34519-21.

19. *Ibid.*

20. James C. Morden, *Historical Monuments and Observatories of Lundy's Lane and Queenston Heights* (Niagara Falls: The Lundy's Lane Historical Society, 1929), 66.

21. *Ibid.*, 71.

22. 14 October 1824, *The Colonial Advocate*; a copy of this issue is in the collection of the Lundy's Lane Museum. Janet Carnochan, *History of Niagara* (Belleville: Mika Publishing, 1973, reprint), 27, 144.

23. Read, *Life and Times ...*, 253.

24. "Proposed Arrangements for the 13th October, 1824," Broadside series, Baldwin Room, Metropolitan Toronto Reference Library.

25. *The Daily Globe*, 14 October 1859.

26. Extract of a letter from John Ball to G. W. Ball, 5 September 1887, displayed with Brock's hat at the Niagara Historical Museum in Niagara-on-the-Lake. Also cited in Kosche, "Relics of Brock ...", footnote 49, 44.

27. Brock Monument Papers, Merritt Papers - package 8, OA, MU 296-97.

28. *America and the Americans* (London, Longman, *et. al*, 1833), 143; this text, written by "a citizen of the world", apparently misquoted the inscription by stating that John McDonald, rather than Macdonell, was entombed with Brock. Morden, *Historical Monuments ...*, 72, also notes the inscription, which is the same inscription (minus the sentence about the tomb) subsequently used on the second monument at Queenston.

29. Harriet Martineau, *Retrospect of Western Travel*, 2 vols. (Saunders and Otley, New York, 1838), 1:100.

30. *Ibid*, 101.

31. *The St. Catharines Journal and Welland Canal, (Niagara District) General Advertiser*, 30 April 1840.

32. *Ibid.*, 25 June 1840, and 30 April 1840.

33. W. Stewart Wallace and W. A. McKay, eds., *The Macmillan Dictionary of Canadian Biography* (Toronto, Macmillan, 1978), 400.

34. *The St. Catharines Journal*, ... 25 June 1840.

35. *Ibid.*, 2 July 1840.

36. *Ibid.*, 16 July 1840. The Ducks is a set of small islands located midway across Lake Ontario just south of the Prince Edward Peninsula.

37. Wallace and McKay, *The Macmillan Dictionary of Canadian Biography*, 470.

38. Details about the meeting are taken from *The St. Catharines Journal*, ... 30 July and 6 August, 1840.

39. *Ibid.*, 6 August.

40. John Symons, ed., *The Battle of Queenston Heights being a Narrative of the Opening of the War of 1812 with notices of the Life of Major-General Sir Isaac Brock, K. B. And description of the Monument Erected to His Memory* (Toronto: Thompson & Co., 1859), 27.

41. List of Designs for a Monument to Brock in 1843, and Payments to Young and runners up Coverdale and Denison in 1843, OA, Brock Monument Papers, 1840-1857, MU 296.

42. Minutes of meeting of Brock Monument Committee, 29 September 1842, Broadsides series, Baldwin Room, Metropolitan Toronto Reference Library.

43. Deputation to the Governor General, 30 September 1842, *ibid*.

44. Minutes of Committee meeting, 24 June 1852, OA, MU 296.

45. "Architectural Notices," *The Canadian Journal*, 1852, 1:22.

46. *Ibid*.

47. Peter J. Stokes, *Old Niagara on the Lake*, (Toronto: University of Toronto Press, 1971), 37.

48. "Architectural Notices: The Brock Monument," *The Canadian Journal*, 1852, 1:41-2.

49. *The Daily Globe*, 14 October 1859.

50. *Ibid*.

51. *Niagara Chronicle,* 13 July 1853, cited in *Notes on Niagara 1759-1860,* 65.

52. *Ibid.,* 29 July 1853, 65. It is probable that the correct date of the issue was Wednesday, 27 July.

53. *The Niagara Mail,* 20 July 1853..

54. Minutes of a meeting chaired by Merritt held on 29 September 1853 at Drummondville quoted in Morden, *Historical Monuments ....* 77-78. A complaint about the lack of publicity and planning was noted in the 20 October issue of *The Niagara Mail,* although a public announcement appeared in *The Mail* as early as 7 September 1853.

55. "The Brock Celebration," *The Niagara Mail,* 20 October 1853. This issue carried extensive coverage of the ceremony.

56. *Ibid.*

57. *Ibid.*

58. *Ibid.*

59. *Ibid.*

60. *Ibid.*

61. Thomas to Street, 16 March 1854, OA, MU 7144.

62. Progress Reports: by William Thomas, 15 October 1855, OA, MU 296, The Brock Monument Papers, 1840-1857; by Building Committee, 22 October 1857; *The Canadian Journal,* May 1856, 203-4.

63. *The Daily Globe,* 14 October 1859.

64. *The Niagara Mail,* 1, 8 and 15 October 1856. *Ibid.,* 27 October 1858.

65. A detailed report of the inauguration was printed in *The Daily Globe,* 14 October.

66. Thomas to McNab, 1 August 1860, OA, Niagara Historical Society Collection, FI9-FI10, 125. A thorn bush on the spot where Brock died is mentioned also in John Howison, *Sketches of Upper Canada* (Edinburgh, Oliver and Boyd, 1821; reprinted Toronto, Coles, 1980), 77.

67. *The Daily Globe,* and *The Daily Standard,* 14 October 1912.

68. *Isaac Brock, Guernsey Man of Canada, Bi-Centenary 1769-1969,* foreword.

Index

Addison, Robert, 4-5
Arthur, Lt. Gov. Sir George, 19, 24-6
Bagot, Gov. Gen. Sir Charles, 28
Ball, George, 14
Brock, James, 14
Brock, John Savery, 9
Brock, Maj. Gen. Sir Isaac
- death, 1-2
- first burial, 3-5
- estate, 6-7
- second burial, 12-16
- third burial, 34-5
- fourth burial, 36-40
Brock, William, 7, 9, 10
Clark, Thomas, 9-10, 14, 16
Cochrane, David, 33, 42
Dickson, Thomas, 9-10, 14, 16
Edward VIII, 47-8
Fitzgibbon, Colonel James, 13
Glegg, Captain John B., 2-7
Guernsey, 7, 8, 48
Hall, Francis, 10, 16-7, 19, 34
Lett, Benjamin, 19-20, 23
Macdonell, Alexander, 4

Macdonell, Donald, 12, 37-8, 47
Macdonell, Duncan, 12
Macdonell, Lt. Col. John, 2-5, 12, 16, 18, 31, 34-35, 37-38
Mackenzie, William Lyon, 12
Maitland, Lt. Gov. Sir Peregrine, 14
McNab, Sir Allan Napier, 26, 28, 37, 44
Merritt, William Hamilton, 26, 37, 39-40, 45, 47
Nichol, Robert, 9-10, 14
Pollock, Robert, 33, 42
Robinson, John Beverley, 25, 26, 47
Sheaffe, Maj. Gen. Sir Roger 2-6
Street, Thomas, 45
Thomas, William, 30, 32-5, 37, 40-2, 45-7
Walcot, Robert, 1
Westmacott, Richard, 7-10
Williams, Gen. Sir William 44
Woodruff, William, 44
Worthington, John, 33, 40-2
Young, Thomas, 26-8, 30